Maths Games

Addition and **Subtraction** Games

Caroline Clissold
Sue Atkinson

HOPSCOTCH
EDUCATIONAL PUBLISHING

1904 307477 7201 73

CONTENTS

Published by
Hopscotch Educational Publishing Ltd.,
Unit 2, the Old Brushworks, 56 Pickwick Rd,
Corsham, Wiltshire, SN13 9BX
Tel: 01249 701701

© 2003 Hopscotch Educational Publishing

Written by Caroline Clissold
Series consultant: Sue Atkinson
Series design: Blade Communications
Illustrated by Susan Hutchison
Printed by Clintplan Limited, Southam

1-904307-4-77

The author would like to thank the many teachers and children from the following schools who trialled these activities:

Bishop Perrin Primary School, Richmond

Sheen Mount Primary School, Richmond

Upton House School, Windsor

Kinsale Middle School, Hellesdon, Norwich

Eye Primary School, Peterborough

Happisburgh First School, Norfolk

Aslacton Primary School, Norfolk

Alpington Primary School, Norfolk

Scarning Primary School, Dereham, Norfolk

West Thurrock Primary School, Essex

St Josephs Primary School, Stanford-le-Hope, Essex

Maths games have been shown to have a positive influence on children's learning and this series of books is designed to raise achievement in your class.

This book of games is suitable for children who are:
- working on learning objectives from about levels 2 or 3 to games suitable for Years 7, 8 and 9 average and high achievers. (For the lower achievers you might need to work from Book 1 which has artwork designed to be suitable for all ages.);
- lower achievers in Key Stage 3. (The artwork has been designed to be suitable for use with older children.);
- in need of more practice with certain key objectives in the National Numeracy Framework.

Using the games

The games are clearly differentiated and are suitable for:
- the whole class to play at the same time;
- working independently in group-work time;
- working with other adults in the classroom;
- use at home as homework or borrowed as part of a maths games library.

It is important to refer to the objectives for the other year groups to give your groups/class a range of differentiated games.

The structure of the book

The chart/contents list on page 5 shows the main learning objective for each of the games.

Each game has a double page of teacher notes followed by photocopiable game boards and/or cards specific to that game. Any resource that is needed for more than one of the games is called a generic sheet; these are at the back of the book.

Also at the back of the book are the rules of the games, presented in such as way that they can be cut out, mounted onto card and used by the children. See page 4 for more information on the rules.

The structure of the teacher's notes

These show the main learning objective, the resources required, how to play the game, variations for the different age ranges and ideas for the plenary session.

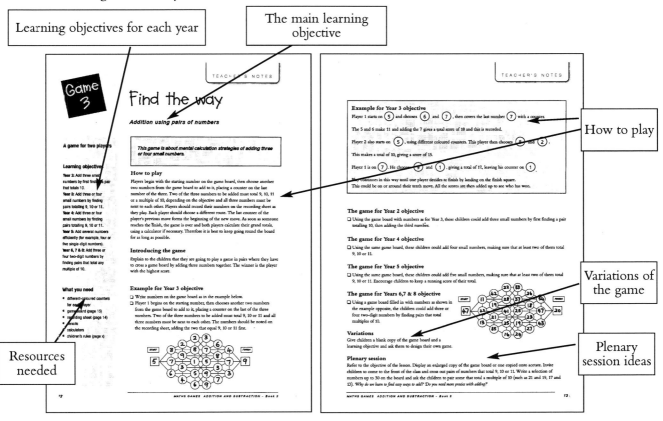

Learning objectives for each year

The main learning objective

How to play

Resources needed

Variations of the game

Plenary session ideas

Preparing the games

The teacher's notes will tell you what you need to play the games and which pages you need to photocopy. You can copy the game boards onto card if you want, or onto paper and laminate them.

The photocopiable number cards, spinners and counters are best copied onto card before they are cut for ease of handling them.

Using the spinners

When you cut out each spinner, cut out the rectangle of card that it is drawn on because having this to hold makes spinning the paper-clip easier.

With one hand, trap the paper-clip with the pencil in the middle of the spinner. Flick the paper clip around with a finger on the other hand. If the clip stops on a line, that player can decide which of the two sections he or she wants.

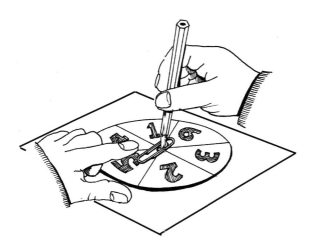

Rules for the games

Rules for the games are explained in the teacher's notes. At the back of the book the rules are presented in such a way that they can be cut out, mounted onto card and used by the children. Some of the games have two versions of the rules. Some of the rules contain blank boxes for the teacher to complete with the relevant numbers to be used in the game. There is a blank rules card which can be used for variations of the games. You might find it helpful for a games library always to stick a copy of the rules on the back of each game, as well as a copy of the rules that can be referred to as the game is played.

Storing the games

Store the games in plastic folders that have been labelled to show the title of the game, the learning objective and the contents of the folder (for example '1 game board, 2 spinners, rules, 4 counters').

A final note

Above all, boost children's self-esteem by your focused assessment questions and your praise and encouragement, so that maths is enjoyed by everyone.

Linking maths concepts to the games in this book

	Game 1	Game 2	Game 3	Game 4	Game 5	Game 6	Game 7	Game 8	Game 9	Game 10	Game 11	Game 12	Game 13
Mental addition strategies	✓	✓	✓	✓	✓	✓	✓	✓	✓	✓	✓	✓	
Addition using pairs of numbers			✓	✓									
Number bonds				✓									
Single digit partitioning					✓								
Addition and subtraction by partitioning and recombining						✓	✓						
Finding a small difference by counting on								✓					
Doubles									✓				
Addition and subtraction by adjusting										✓			
Addition and subtraction with inversions						✓			✓		✓	✓	
Choosing an appropriate mental strategy	✓	✓											✓

Shape snakes

Mental addition strategies

This game is for teaching children to use efficient strategies, such as putting the largest number first and adding on.

A game for two players

Learning objectives

Year 1: Begin to recognise that addition can be done in any order.

Year 2: Using the knowledge that addition can be done in any order, begin to add three small numbers by putting the largest first.

Year 3: Extend understanding that more than two numbers can be added.

Year 4: Add 3 two-digit multiples of 10.

Year 5: Add decimal numbers, for example 6.8 + 2.2.

Year 6, 7 & 8: Add several decimal numbers.

What you need

- a recording sheet (page 8)
- 22 numbered hexagonal card shapes (page 9)
- pencils and paper
- children's rules (page 82)

How to play

This game is similar in principle to dominoes. Each player takes it in turn to choose one of their number cards to place down after a previous number card in order to make a total within a given range of numbers.

Introducing the game

Tell the children that they are going to play a game in pairs involving adding in their head. Explain that the aim of the game is to make a picture of a snake using hexagons while trying to make the target score by adding. Revise addition strategies, such as putting the largest number first, but stress that they can use any strategy. Although the game focuses on mental strategies, encourage jottings where needed but discourage algorithms.

Example for Year 5 objective

Prepare 22 hexagonal cards, each with one of the following numbers written on it: 6.4, 6.8, 7.3, 7.9, 8.2, 8.7, 9.1 and 9.6 (Repeat these numbers until all 22 cards are filled.)

❏ The aim of the game is to make a total within the range of numbers from 14 to 16 with two cards. (See the example at the top of the facing page.)

❏ One child shuffles and deals ten cards to each player.

❏ One of the spare cards is placed face up on the table. Player 1 looks at her cards and chooses one that she thinks, when added to the one face up, will give a total of between 14 and 16. She places the card alongside the first, writes down her calculation on the recording sheet and, if successful, scores a point.

❏ Player 2 then chooses from his cards one that he thinks will total between 14 and 16 when added to the last card placed on the table. He places that card alongside Player 1's card, so that they begin to form the shape of a snake.

❏ Play continues in this way until all the hexagon cards have been used. If it is not possible to score within the range of 14 to 16, the player must still place a card and record the calculation but not score a point. The winner is the player with the most points once all the shapes have been placed.

In this example, the hexagon card with 6.4 written on it was placed face up on the table. Player 1 placed a hexagon worth 8.2, which totals 14.6, so she scored a point. Player 2 placed a hexagon worth 6.8, which, when added to the previous number (8.2) totalled 15. Player 1 placed a hexagon worth 7.9 which, when added to the previous number (6.8) totalled 16.7. This is not within the target range, so Player 1 does not score. (You could include the additional bonus that if a player makes a total of one of the whole numbers, they score an extra point.)

6.4   6.8   9.1
   8.2   7.9

Example for Year 1 objective

❏ Play as for Year 5 but the numbers on the cards should be 3, 4, 5, 6 and 7, and the target range 9, 10 and 11.

Example for Year 2 objective

❏ Play as for Year 5 but the numbers on the cards should be 5, 6, 7, 8, 9 and 10, and the target range 14, 15 and 16.

Example for Year 3 objective

❏ These children will be adding three lots of numbers together for this objective, so instead of having one card face up at the beginning, you need two placed side by side. The first player chooses a number to add to these two to make the target total. The second player will add theirs to the first player's and total their card and the previous two cards. The numbers on the cards should be 6, 7, 8, 9, 10 and 11 and the target range 24 to 28.

Example for Year 4 objective

❏ These children play as for Year 3 (adding 3 numbers) but the numbers on the cards should be 20, 30, 40, 50, 60 and 70 and the target range multiples of 10 from 120 to 160.

Example for Years 6, 7 & 8 objective

❏ These children play as for Year 3 (adding 3 numbers) but the numbers on the cards should be 6.4, 6.8, 7.3, 7.9, 8.2, 8.7, 9.1 and 9.6 and the target range 21 to 25.
❏ Extend the game by using two places of decimals, first adding 2, then 3 cards. For example, 1.46 + 2.91 + 1.06. The children might need to make jottings.

Variation

❏ Vary the numbers and ranges that are used. For example, 26.7 , 27.3 with a target range of 54 to 56.

Plenary session

❏ Discuss with the children the strategies they used to work out the calculations. Did they always put the largest number in their head and then add on the other? Did they use near doubles (18 + 17: double 18 and then take off 1, or double 17 and add 1)? Did they partition (18 + 17: 18 + 2 to make 20 and then add on the 15 left)? Did they add 19 by adding 20 and taking away 1? Choose a few examples and discuss the efficiency of these methods.

Names:

Recording sheet

Player 2

Number taken	Numbers to be added	Total	Score

Final score

Player 1

Number taken	Numbers to be added	Total	Score

Final score

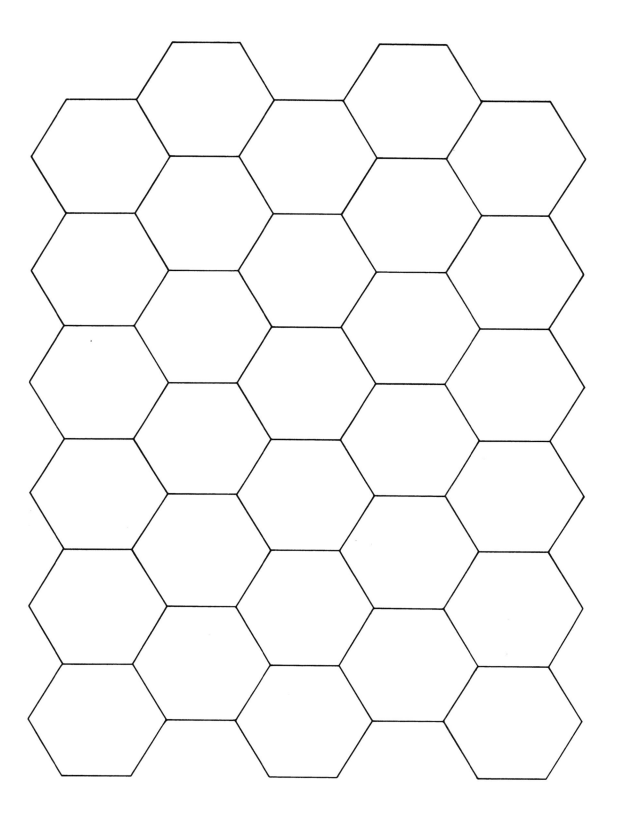

Notes for teachers: Cut out these shapes and write numbers in each one as suggested in the various year objectives on pages 6 and 7.

Cover the numbers

Addition and subtraction of one- and two-digit numbers

A game for two to four players

Learning objectives

Year 2: Add/subtract a single-digit number to/from any two-digit number, with jottings if needed.

Year 3: Add/ subtract a pair of two-digit numbers, with jottings if needed.

Year 4: Add/subtract any pair of two-digit numbers mentally, including crossing the tens boundary.

Year 5: Add/subtract a pair of decimal fractions each with units and tenths.

Year 6, 7 & 8: Add/subtract a pair of decimal fractions, both less than one and up to two decimal places.

What you need

- Generic sheets 1–8, 12–14, 16
- counters
- a timer
- paper, pencils and number lines for jottings
- children's rules (page 82)

> This game gives children experience with choosing for themselves an efficient calculation strategy.

How to play
The aim of the game is to cover as many squares as possible on the game board in a given time, by answering addition or subtraction calculations.

Introducing the game
Tell the children that they are going to play a game involving adding and subtracting mentally, making jottings (for example, on blank number lines) where necessary. Specify the amount of time that will be allowed for the game and do some examples together using a number line.

Example for Year 3 objective
Prepare the two-digit number cards from Generic sheet 6 and Spinner 1 on Generic sheet 1. Each player needs counters in their own colour. For this game the 100 board on Generic sheet 2 is the game board (you might want to enlarge it).

❑ Set a time limit; for example, 10 minutes.
❑ Shuffle the two-digit cards and place them face down in the middle of the table.
❑ Player 1 spins the + or – spinner and takes two cards from the two-digit cards pile. If the operation is +, he adds the two numbers together; if it is – he takes the smallest number away from the largest. He can make jottings if he needs to. If the resulting number is on the game board, he can cover it with one of his colour counters. If the number has already been covered or is not on the game board, he can't use it.
❑ The next players then have their turns in the same way.
❑ Play continues until the time is up.
❑ The winner is the player with the most counters on the game board at the end of the game.

See the top of the facing page for an example of how the game should be played.

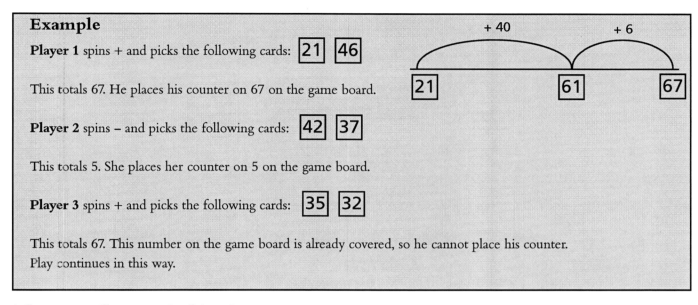

Example

Player 1 spins + and picks the following cards: [21] [46]

This totals 67. He places his counter on 67 on the game board.

Player 2 spins – and picks the following cards: [42] [37]

This totals 5. She places her counter on 5 on the game board.

Player 3 spins + and picks the following cards: [35] [32]

This totals 67. This number on the game board is already covered, so he cannot place his counter.
Play continues in this way.

The game for Year 2 objective

❑ These children play as for Year 3, but they use the digit cards from Generic sheet 4, the two-digit cards from Generic sheet 5 and the + and – spinner on Generic Sheet 1. You can use the blanks on this Generic sheet 5 to make your own number cards.

The game for Year 4 objective

❑ These children play as for Year 3, using the 100 board, but use the cards from Generic sheets 7 and 8 and any other numbers you want using the blanks on Generic sheet 5. Encourage the children to work in their heads initially and then to check using jottings, for example on number lines.

The game for Year 5 objective (also suitable for Year 6)

❑ These children play as for Year 3, but use Generic sheet as 3 the game board and the one-decimal place cards on Generic sheet 12 or 13 to add or subtract.

The game for Years 6, 7 and 8 objective

❑ Use the same basic rules as for the Year 3 example, but use Generic sheet 3 as the game board and the two-decimal place cards on Generic sheet 14 to add or subtract. The children then round their answers to the nearest tenth. For example, if their answer is 4.69, they need to round it to 4.7 and place it on the 4.7 square on the board.

Variation

For extension and support you could:
❑ ask the children to work together to see how many numbers they can cover;
❑ use place value cards with the 10s in one bag and 1s in another (Generic sheet 16).

Plenary session

❑ Use the relevant game board copied onto acetate and play this game on an OHP. Divide the class into four teams and have a time limit of six minutes. Discuss with the children the strategies they used to solve the calculations. Ask *'Was that a good strategy for those numbers?', 'Would anyone have done it a different way?'* and *'What do you need more help with?'*

Find the way

Addition using pairs of numbers

A game for two players

Learning objectives

Year 2: Add three small numbers by first finding a pair that totals 10.
Year 3: Add three or four small numbers by finding pairs totalling 9, 10 or 11.
Year 4: Add three or four small numbers by finding pairs totalling 9, 10 or 11.
Year 5: Add several numbers efficiently (for example, four or five single-digit numbers).
Year 6, 7 & 8: Add three or four two-digit numbers by finding pairs that total any multiple of 10.

What you need

- different-coloured counters for each player
- a game board (page 15)
- a recording sheet (page 14)
- pencils
- calculators
- children's rules (page 83)

> This game is about mental calculation strategies of adding three or four small numbers.

How to play

Players begin with the starting number on the game board, then choose another two numbers from the game board to add to it, placing a counter on the last number of the three. Two of the three numbers to be added must total 9, 10, 11 or a multiple of 10, depending on the objective and all three numbers must be next to each other. Players should record their numbers on the recording sheet as they play. Each player should choose a different route. The last counter of the player's previous move forms the beginning of the new move. As soon as someone reaches the finish, the game is over and both players calculate their grand totals, using a calculator if necessary. Therefore it is best to keep going round the board for as long as possible.

Introducing the game

Explain to the children that they are going to play a game in pairs where they have to cross a game board by adding three numbers together. The winner is the player with the highest score.

Example for Year 3 objective

❏ Write numbers on the game board as in the example below.
❏ Player 1 begins on the starting number, then chooses another two numbers from the game board to add to it, placing a counter on the last of the three numbers. Two of the three numbers to be added must total 9, 10 or 11 and all three numbers must be next to each other. The numbers should be noted on the recording sheet, adding the two that equal 9, 10 or 11 first.

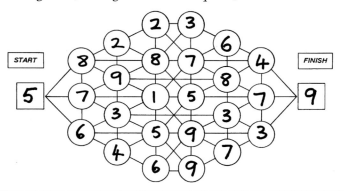

The game for Year 2 objective

❏ Using the game board with numbers as for Year 3, these children could add three small numbers by first finding a pair totalling 10, then adding the third number.

The game for Year 4 objective

❏ Using the same game board, these children could add four small numbers, making sure that at least two of them total 9, 10 or 11.

The game for Year 5 objective

❏ Using the same game board, these children could add five small numbers, making sure that at least two of them total 9, 10 or 11. Encourage children to keep a running score of their total.

The game for Years 6,7 & 8 objective

❏ Using a game board filled in with numbers as shown in the example opposite, the children could add three or four two-digit numbers by finding pairs that total multiples of 10.

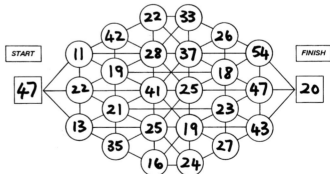

Variations

❏ Give children a blank copy of the game board and a
❏ learning objective and ask them to design their own game.

Plenary session

❏ Refer to the objective of the lesson. Display an enlarged copy of the game board or one copied onto acetate. Invite children to come to the front of the class and cross out pairs of numbers that total 9, 10 or 11. Write a selection of numbers up to 30 on the board and ask the children to pair some that total a multiple of 10 (such as 21 and 19, 17 and 13). *Why do we learn to find easy ways to add? Do you need more practice with adding?*

Names:

Recording sheet

Player 1

Numbers chosen	Total score
Grand Total:	

Player 2

Numbers chosen	Total score
Grand Total:	

Game board

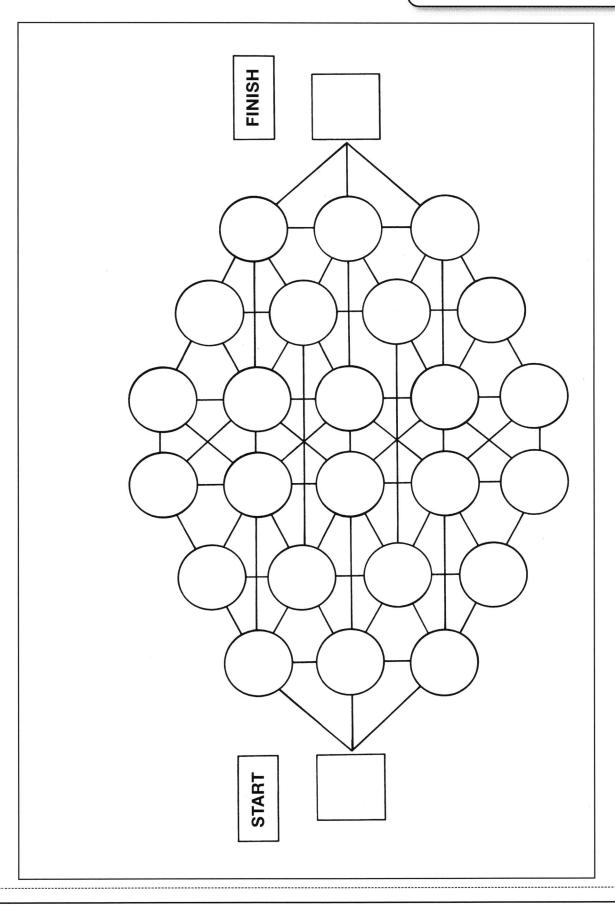

FINISH

START

✂ --

Notes for teachers: This game board is for use with the all the objectives as suggested on pages 12 and 13.

Game 4

Stars in your eyes

Number bonds

A game for two players or small groups

Learning objectives

Year 2: Know by heart all pairs of numbers that total 20.
Year 3: Know by heart all pairs of multiples of 5 with a total of 100.
Year 4: Know by heart all number pairs that total 100.
Year 5: Derive quickly decimals that total 1.
Year 6, 7 & 8: Derive quickly decimals that total any whole number.

What you need

- Generic sheets 1 and 4–9
- a game board for each player (page 18)
- pencils
- appropriate number cards
- counters
- spinners, dice
- children's rules (page 83)

This game helps children to learn by heart the addition of pairs of numbers.

How to play

Each player has a star game board, completed with the numbers you are addressing. They take one number card from a pack and if they can use it to match with one on the board to make the target number, they cover that number. The winner is the first to cover all their numbers on their star.

Introducing the game

Tell the children that this game will help to reinforce learning the pairs of numbers that make a specific total (depending on their age and level of achievement). Explain that they are going to play in pairs or small groups, and that the aim of the game is to be the first to cover all the numbers on their own game board.

Example for Year 3 objective

❑ You need a pack of cards with numbers from 5 to 95 that are multiples of 5 (Generic sheet 6).
❑ Give each child a star game board. Ask them to write in the spaces numbers from 5 to 95 that are multiples of 5, as in the examples below.
❑ The children then take it in turn to pick a card. If the number on the card can be paired with one of the numbers on the child's star on their game board to make 100, the player can cover up that number on their game board with a counter. See the example at the top of the facing page.
❑ After each go, players should replace their cards at the bottom of the pile.

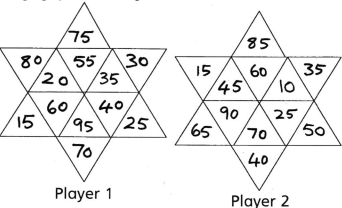

Player 1   Player 2

Example for Year 3 objective

Player 1 picks up a card with the number 80 on it. To make 100, the partner to that is 20, which is on her star, so she covers 20 with a counter.

Player 2 picks 65 and so can cover 35 on his board.

Player 1 picks 15. There is no 85 on her star, so she cannot place a counter on the board.

Player 2 picks 30 and so can cover 70. And so on.

Example for Year 2 objective

❑ The aim here is to make pairs that total 20. You could use the cards from Generic sheet 5 (10–20) and digit cards on Generic sheet 4 (0–9). Players 1 and 2 fill in their stars with numbers from 1 to 20. They then take it in turns to pick up a card from the pack which is face down. So, for example, 13 is turned over and 7 is covered.

Example for Year 4 objective

❑ These children can play the game using cards from 0–100 with the game board having random numbers to 100. The aim is to make 100. Use the cards from Generic sheets 7, 8 and 9. You can show the children which random numbers they are using before they write in their star numbers.

Example for Year 5 objective

❑ These children should write decimal numbers on their stars, such as 2.3 and 4.4. Each player could use two stars if you prefer as this gives a greater probability that a number can be covered. The aim is to make 10. Use Spinner 2 on Generic sheet 1 (or throw two 1–6 dice) and spin twice. For example, a spin of 3 and then 4 makes 3.4 (or 4.3). So, if 6.6 (or 5.7) is on their star it can be covered. Decide which dice/spinner is to be used before the numbers are written on the star.

Example for Year 6, 7 & 8 objective

❑ Use the game in 'Variations'.

Variations

❑ For confident children only at first. Organise the children into evenly matched pairs. They fill in one or two stars with whole numbers. They choose a star number, such as 6. They throw three 1–6 or 1–10 dice to make a decimal number, such as 4.15. Both players race to write down the decimal that makes 4.15 up to 6. The fastest covers the 6 with their counter. The winner is the player with the most counters on the stars at the end.

❑ Challenge the children to make their own cards so that they can write the numbers on their star and cover a number every time. They can choose their own target numbers to make.

❑ Try to make a subtraction game!

Plenary session

❑ Choose a different target number, such as 80 for Year 3 and 1000 for Year 4. Fill in two stars and play the game in two teams. Choose a target number, such as 100 or 1. Call out a number, such as 63 or 0.3, and ask the class to work out how many to add to make the target. Ask *Why do you think it is important to be able to add quickly like this?*

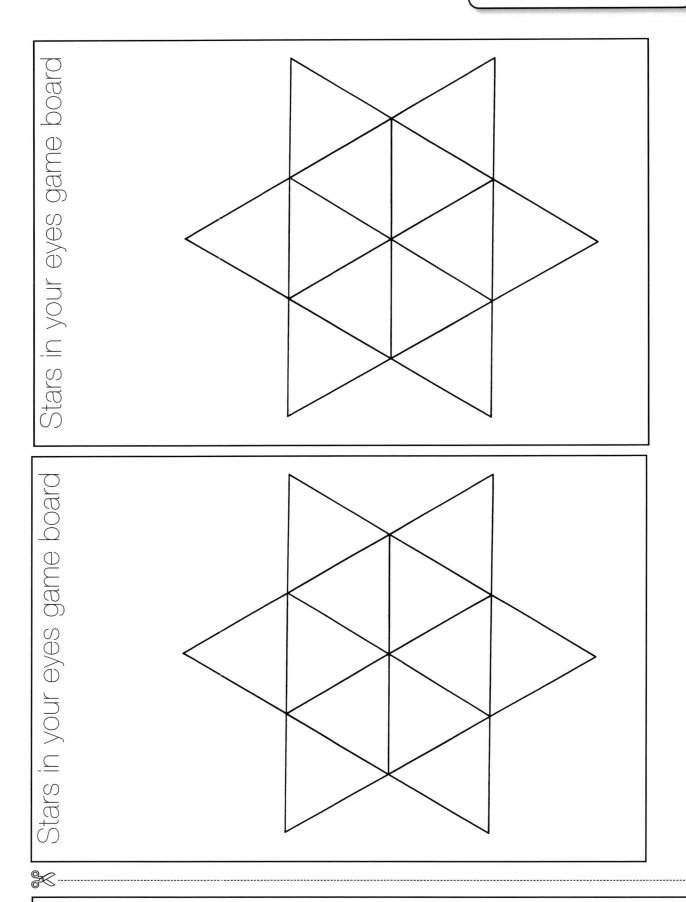

Stars in your eyes game board

Stars in your eyes game board

Notes for teachers: This game board is for use with all the objectives as suggested on page 16 and 17.
Each child has one star.

Game 5

What's left?

Single-digit partitioning

A game for two to four players

Learning objectives

Year 2: Partition a number into something and a bit when adding to a number up to 50.

Year 3: Partition a number into something and a bit when adding to a two- or three-digit number.

Years 4, 5 & 6: Revision of Year 3 objectives, to include decimals.

Years 6, 7 & 8: Partitioning decimals when adding.

What you need

- number cards
- a game board (pages 21 and 22)
- a recording sheet (page 23)
- counters
- Generic sheets 6–11, 13
- children's rules (page 84)

> This game helps children to add mentally, using the strategy of partitioning.

How to play

A pack of number cards suitable for the children's achievement is placed face down. Players put their counters on the first number square on the game board. They take turns to turn over a card and add it to the number in the first square. But they must do this by partitioning the number in the square into two numbers to make the number on the card up to the next multiple of 10. The number that is left over is the number of moves the player can make along the board. If one of the additions does not leave anything left over, the player cannot move their counter. The winner is the first player to generate the right number to reach 'home'. Players can record their calculations on the recording sheet on page 23.

Introducing the game

Tell the children that they are going to play a game that will help them to learn to add mentally a single-digit number to a two- or three-digit number. They are to use the strategy of partitioning the single-digit number to make the next multiple of 10. Do some examples with them; for example, 26 + 7. To make the 26 up to the next multiple of 10 add 4 (26 + 4 = 30) and then add the 3 (30 + 3 = 33).

Example for Year 3 objective

❑ Use the game board on page 21 and the number cards on Generic sheets 9 and 10. You may want the children to record their calculation on the recording sheet on page 23.

❑ Player 1 turns over the card 159. He must add the number in the first square, which is 6 **but he must first make the next number that is a multiple of 10.** So, he partitions the 6 into 1 and 5. The 1 makes the 159 up to 160 and the 5 is the left-over number that gives a total of 165. So Player 1 moves his counter 5 places forward on to the 8 square.

❑ Player 2 picks 28 and has to add 6, so she partitions 6 into 4 and 2. She adds the 2 to the 28 to make 30. There is 4 left over to make 34 so she moves her counter 4 places forward.

❑ Player 1 picks 211 and has to add 8. This can't be partitioned to make the next multiple of 10, so he can't move.

See the top of the facing page for a demonstration of these moves.

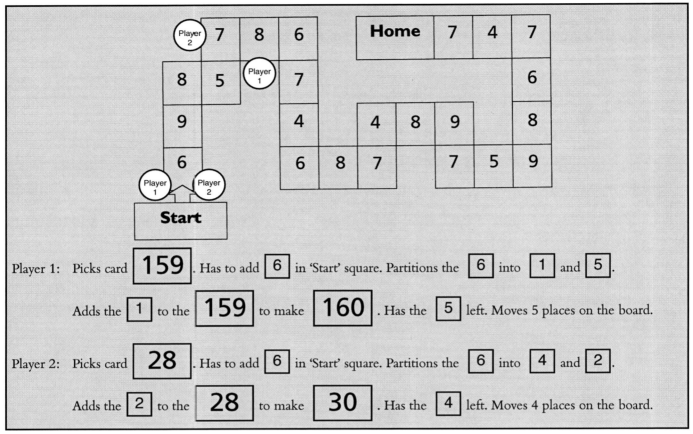

Example for Year 2 objective

❏ These children play the same game but using game cards just of two-digit numbers from Generic sheets 7 and 9.

Example for Years 4, 5 and 6 objectives

❏ These children play the same game but using any two-, three- or four-digit numbers on Generic sheets 6–11. Alternatively, these children could play the game using decimal cards. Use the cards on Generic sheet 13. Explain that the numbers on the game board are tenths, therefore 9 represents 0.9. You might want to write the 0. before each number. If a child picks card 3.4, he must add that to 0.9. This makes 4.3 and he can move three places.

Example for Years 6, 7 and 8 objectives

❏ Use the blank number cards on Generic sheet 5 to make decimals with tenths and hundredths, such as 6.37. Change the game board also, so 6 could become 0.69. Adding 0.69 and 6.37, the player partitions the 7 into 1 and 6. 0.69 + 0.01 is 0.70 and the 6 in 6.36 is left over so that player moves 6 spaces.

Variations

❏ Give the children Game board 2 (page 22) and blank number cards (Generic sheet 5) or spinners or dice and ask them to make their own version of the game.

Plenary session

❏ Write a number on the board and call out a single-digit number. Ask the children to work out what will be left after partitioning the single-digit number to make the one on the board up to the next 10. They then need to hold up the appropriate digit card from their selection to identify the left-over number. Of course, the numbers chosen will have to cross the 10s boundary, but you could include a few that won't as 'trick questions'. Ask *Do you find partitioning a useful strategy when you add mentally?*

Game board – 1

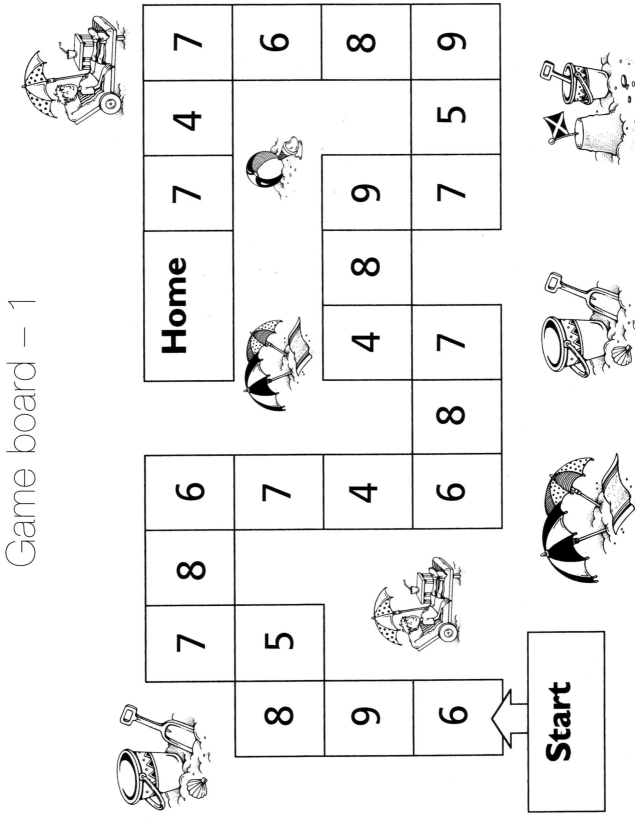

Notes for teachers: This game board is for use with the all the objectives as suggested on pages 19 and 20.

Game board – 2

Home

Start

✂ -

Notes for teachers: This game board is for use with the game suggested in Variations on page 20.

Names:_____

Recording sheet

Number picked	How many to add on?	How many to next multiple?	What's left over?

Game 6

Hurdles

Addition and subtraction by partitioning and recombining

A game for two to six players

Learning objectives

Year 2: Partition additions into tens and units, then recombine.

Year 3: Partition into tens and units, add or subtract, then recombine.

Year 4: Partition into tens and units, adding/subtracting the tens first, and recombine.

Year 5, 6, 7 & 8: Partition into hundreds, tens and units, adding/ subtracting the most significant digit first.

What you need

- Generic sheets 1, 16–17
- a game board (the game board shown [page 25] is for three players, but an additional copy can be made to allow up to six players)
- counters
- pencil and paper for jottings
- children's rules (page 84)

> This game helps children to add mentally, using the strategy of partitioning numbers and then recombining them.

How to play

The aim of the game is for players to do additions and subtractions that enable them to jump the hurdles on the game board to win the race. Sets of place value cards are placed face down, all the 10s in one pile and the 1s in another pile. The highest total (if addition is spun) or lowest total (if subtraction is spun) will win. Each player picks a card from each set and makes a number with them. They repeat this to make a second number. They add their two numbers together (or subtract them) by partitioning them. They then recombine them mentally to give a total. The winner jumps a hurdle on their race track, if the other players agree they are right.

Introducing the game

Tell the children that this game will help them to learn to add or subtract mentally by using the strategy of partitioning tens and units numbers and then recombining them. For all age groups, you might want to introduce the game just with addition to ensure they understand it. Encourage them to make jottings to aid mental calculation.

Example for Year 3 objectives

❑ Using tens and units place value cards, Player 1 picks the cards 20 and 3 and combines them to make 23. She then picks 40 and 7 and combines them to make 47. Spinner 1 is spun to + so the numbers are to be added. She adds the 20 and the 40 to make 60. She adds the 3 and the 7 to make 10. Finally, she adds the 60 and the 10 and calculates that the total is 70.

❑ With the spinner on +, Player 2 picks 30 and 5, then 10 and 9 and makes 35 and 19. He adds the 30 and the 10 to make 40 and then the 5 and the 9 to make 14. He then adds the 40 and the 10 to make 50 and adds on the 4 for a total of 54.

❑ Player 1 wins the round and makes a jump over the hurdle.

❑ In the second round they do the same but this time spin a subtraction so they subtract the smaller number from the larger. The player with the lowest total jumps the hurdle.

See the top of the facing page for a demonstration of this.

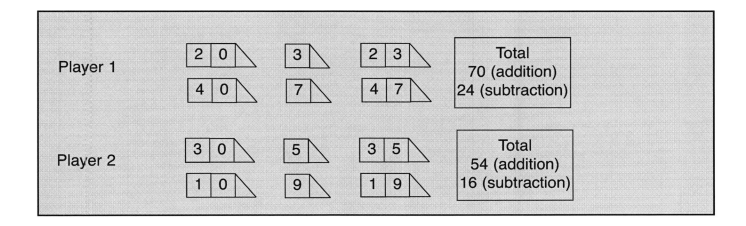

Example for Year 2 objectives

❏ These children should only use addition to partition into tens and units, then recombine.

Example for Year 4 objectives

❏ These children should play the game as described for Year 3 but have three lots of 10s place value cards and three lots of 1s place value cards and do only addition. So they will be adding 3 two-digit numbers by partitioning and recombining. The player with the highest total jumps the hurdle.

❏ For a more challenging game, they could subtract the three numbers aiming for the highest total. For example, Player 1 makes the numbers 34, 64 and 73. 64 – 34 = 30. 73 – 30 = 43. Any other combination of subtractions gives a lower number.

Example for Year 5, 6, 7 & 8 objectives

❏ Let the children partition into hundreds, tens and units. They can play addition or subtraction and partition two or three lots of numbers.

Variations

❏ You could adapt the game to playing with decimals, so cards 200, 30 and 4 could mean 2.34. Alternatively, they could play with three 1–6 or 1–10 dice.

Plenary session

❏ Select cards as in the game and ask individuals or pairs to explain exactly what they are doing. Pay particular attention to calculations where a boundary is crossed, such as 49 + 37 or 51 – 26. How do they do it? The children will have a range of mental methods for solving these problems. Encourage them to jot down their calculations, such as on number lines. Ask *'What is another way you could have done that calculation?'*, *'Why is 51 – 37 more difficult to do than 57 – 31?'*, *'What jottings did you make?'*, *'Who else used a number line?'* and *'Who did it a different way?'*

Game board

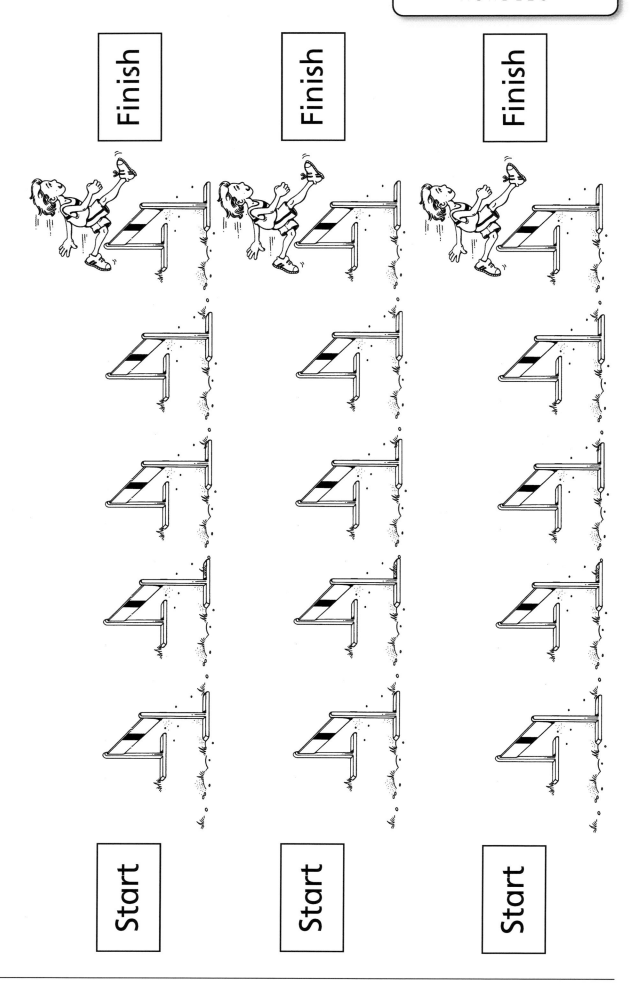

Target numbers

Partitioning and recombining

A game for two to four players

Learning objectives

Year 2: Combine numbers that have been partitioned into tens and units, finding small differences.
Year 3: Combine numbers that have been partitioned into tens and units, finding small differences.
Year 4: Combine numbers that have been partitioned into hundreds, tens and units, finding small differences.
Year 5: Combine numbers that have been partitioned into thousands, hundreds, tens and units, finding small differences.
Year 6, 7 & 8: Partitioning and recombining decimals.

What you need

- a game board (page 9))
- number cards (Generic sheets 4–10
- place value cards (Generic sheets 16 and 17)
- counters
- a number line
- children's rules (page 85)

This game helps children to use the strategy of partitioning numbers and then recombining them and finding small differences.

How to play

The aim of the game is to reach the dartboard first using a target number card and place value cards. Place the two sets of cards in piles face down. Player 1 picks a number from the target number set. Then each player picks place value cards and combines them. They then calculate the difference between their number and the target number. The player who has made the number closest to the target number (either higher or lower) can move their arrow counter one space along the game board. If that player can tell everyone how close they are to the target number, they can move another space along the board. The cards are put back and mixed up. Player 2 picks a new target number card and play continues. Play continues until someone reaches the target. Players can refer to a number line to help them whenever necessary.

Introducing the game

Tell the children that this game will help them to learn to partition and recombine numbers. Explain that the aim is to get their arrow counter to the dartboard first.

Example for Year 3 objective

- ❏ Use target cards from 10 to 99.
- ❏ Player 1 picks the target card 34.
- ❏ Each of four players picks a tens and a units place value card and combines them to make a two-digit number. When combined these are 54, 23, 42 and 41. They find the difference between their number and the target number.
- ❏ 41 is the closest to the target number, so Player 4 moves one space along the board. Player 4 also knows that he is 7 away from the target number, so moves on one more space.
- ❏ The cards are replaced.
- ❏ Player 2 picks the target number 74. The numbers made are 82, 27, 12 and 63. Player 1 is closest and knows by how much so moves two spaces.

See top of the facing page for a demonstration of this.

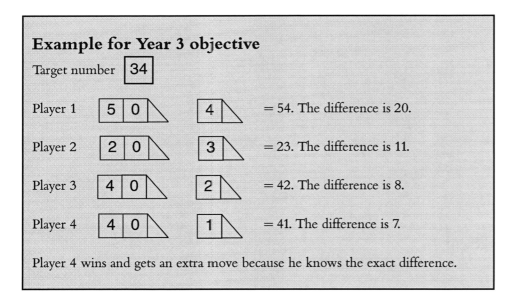

Example for Year 3 objective

Target number $\boxed{34}$

Player 1 $\boxed{5 \mid 0}$ $\boxed{4}$ = 54. The difference is 20.

Player 2 $\boxed{2 \mid 0}$ $\boxed{3}$ = 23. The difference is 11.

Player 3 $\boxed{4 \mid 0}$ $\boxed{2}$ = 42. The difference is 8.

Player 4 $\boxed{4 \mid 0}$ $\boxed{1}$ = 41. The difference is 7.

Player 4 wins and gets an extra move because he knows the exact difference.

Example for Year 2 objective

❑ This group can play the game using target cards from 10 to 50 and place value cards for tens and units. Players mark their target on a number line. They work out where their two-digit number goes on the number line so they can see who is closest to the target.

Example for Year 4 objective

❑ This group can play the game using hundreds, tens and units place value cards and targets from 100 to 500.

Example for Year 5 objective

❑ These children can play the game using target numbers from 100 to 1000 and place value cards up to 900.

Example for Year 6, 7 & 8 objective

❑ For these children the target cards can be from 1–10. Using sets of digit cards (Generic sheet 4), players take three of them and make a decimal, such as 2.14.

Variations

❑ Play with two or three dice rather than cards.

Plenary session

❑ Write some numbers on the board one at a time. Give the children a scenario, such as *Robin shoots two arrows and one of them hits a double on the target. The total is 43. What might have been the numbers he hit?* Ask for as many solutions as possible – double 20 plus 3, double 18 plus 7 and so on. Ask the children to explain their answer by partitioning the numbers, adding them and then recombining. Invite a few of them to write their explanations on the board.

Game board and counters

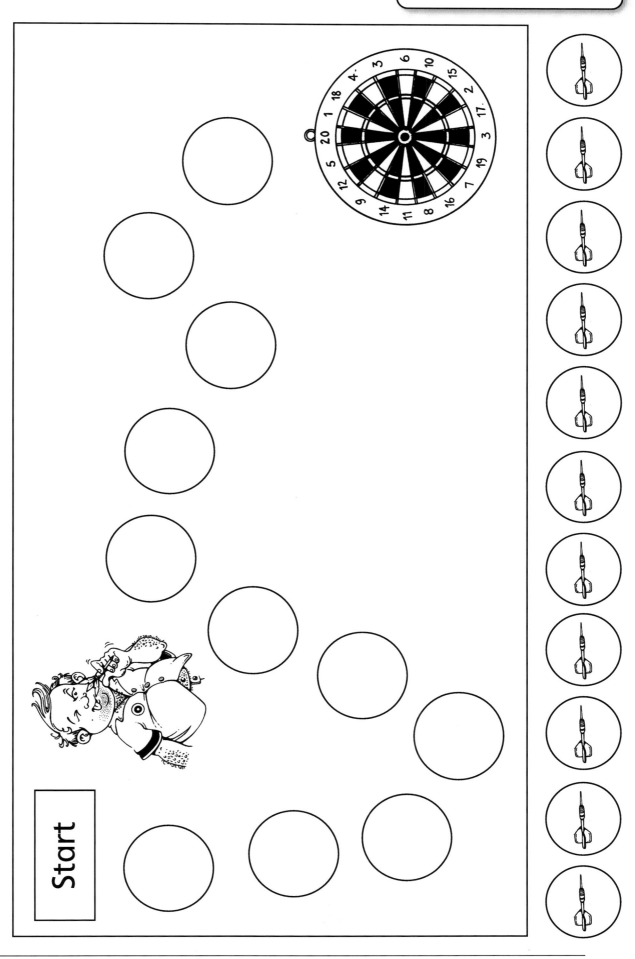

Start

Lost in space!

Finding a small difference by counting on

> This game helps children to find differences, crossing boundaries.

A game for two to six players

Learning objectives

Year 2: Find a small difference by counting up crossing the tens boundary, for example 42 – 39.
Year 3: Find a small difference by counting up crossing the hundreds boundary.
Year 4: Find a small difference by counting up crossing the thousands boundary.
Year 5: Find differences by counting up from one decimal place through to the next whole.
Year 6, 7 & 8: Find differences by counting up from two decimal places through to the next tenth.

What you need

- a game board (page 32)
- spinners (pages 33 and 34 and Generic sheet 1)
- spaceship counters
- a number line, paper and pencil
- children's rules (page 85)

How to play

Using the relevant spinners for the group, players spin two spinners and then work out the difference between the two numbers by counting up from the smaller number, using a number line to check if necessary. They then move their counter that number of spaces along the game board. Play then passes to the next player. They keep playing in this way until one player's counter reaches Earth. You could make the game more difficult by making the target Earth only achievable if they have the exact number to land on it. If they need, for example, a 5 to land on it and their difference is a 7 they must go to Earth and then back two spaces. Their target then is to get a 2.

Introducing the game

Tell the children that they are going to play a game to help them learn to find differences by counting on from the smaller number to the larger. Suggest that they are lost in space and the aim is to be the first player to get their spaceship back to Earth. Show them how to use the spinners. Demonstrate how to draw an 'empty' number line and use it to find differences.

Example for Year 3 objective

❑ Using the spinners from pages 33 and 34, Player 1 spins the two spinners which land on 194 and 205.
❑ Player 1 works out the difference by counting up from the smallest number, using a number line if necessary. The difference is 11, so she moves 11 spaces along the track.
❑ Player 2 spins 199 and 203, and so moves 4 spaces.
❑ Player 3 spins 198 and 205, and moves 7 spaces.
❑ The game continues until someone reaches Earth.

See the demonstration of this on the facing page.

Example for Year 3 objective

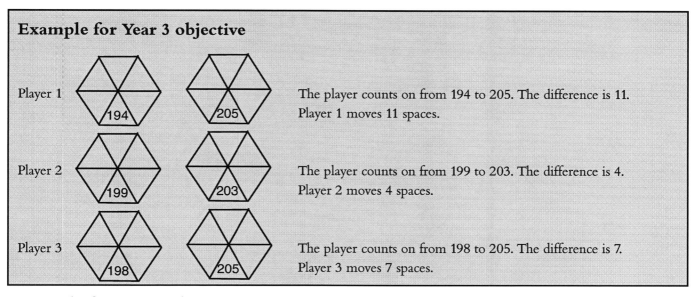

Player 1   194   205   The player counts on from 194 to 205. The difference is 11. Player 1 moves 11 spaces.

Player 2   199   203   The player counts on from 199 to 203. The difference is 4. Player 2 moves 4 spaces.

Player 3   198   205   The player counts on from 198 to 205. The difference is 7. Player 3 moves 7 spaces.

Example for Year 2 objective

❏ Use the set of spinners on page 33. The children have to find small differences by counting along a number line, crossing the tens boundary, for example, 31 – 28. The answer is 3 and so the player moves three spaces along the board.

Example for Year 4 objective

❏ Let the children use spinners on page 33 for crossing the thousands barrier. So, if one player throws 2997 and 3003, they subtract the first number from the second, get a difference of 6 and move 6 spaces along the board.

Example for Year 5 objective

❏ These children can use the spinners on page 34 which include decimals to tenths. They would have to move along the game board by the number of difference of tenths they find.

Example for Year 6, 7 & 8 objective

❏ The children can play the same game but using the spinners on page 34 for decimal 100th. They move along the game board one space for every difference of 100th.

Variations

❏ Let the children use the blank spinners on page 34 to make different numbers. For a shorter game players don't need the exact number to finish.

Plenary session

❏ As a progression, make two spinners using the blank ones on page 34 and fill them in with the numbers 311 to 316 on one and 661 to 666 on the other. Ask the children to come out to the front and spin them and then work out the difference between the two numbers. Ask a volunteer to explain the answer on a number line. Discuss how many 100s barriers are being crossed. So, the difference between 315 and 664 would be explained in this way:

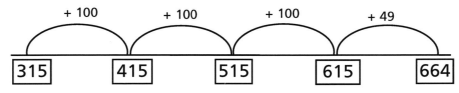

+ 100   + 100   + 100   + 49

315   415   515   615   664

Game board and counters

Year 2

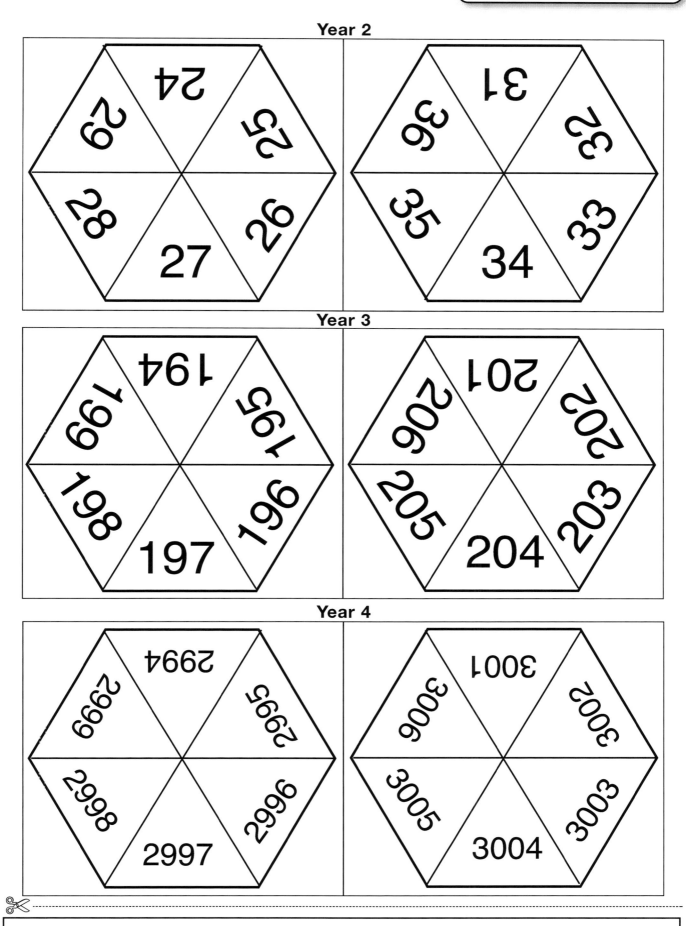

Year 3

Year 4

Notes for teachers: These spinners are for use with the objectives for Years 2, 3 and 4.

MATHS GAMES **ADDITION AND SUBTRACTION – Book 2**　　　　　　PHOTOCOPIABLE　　33

Year 5

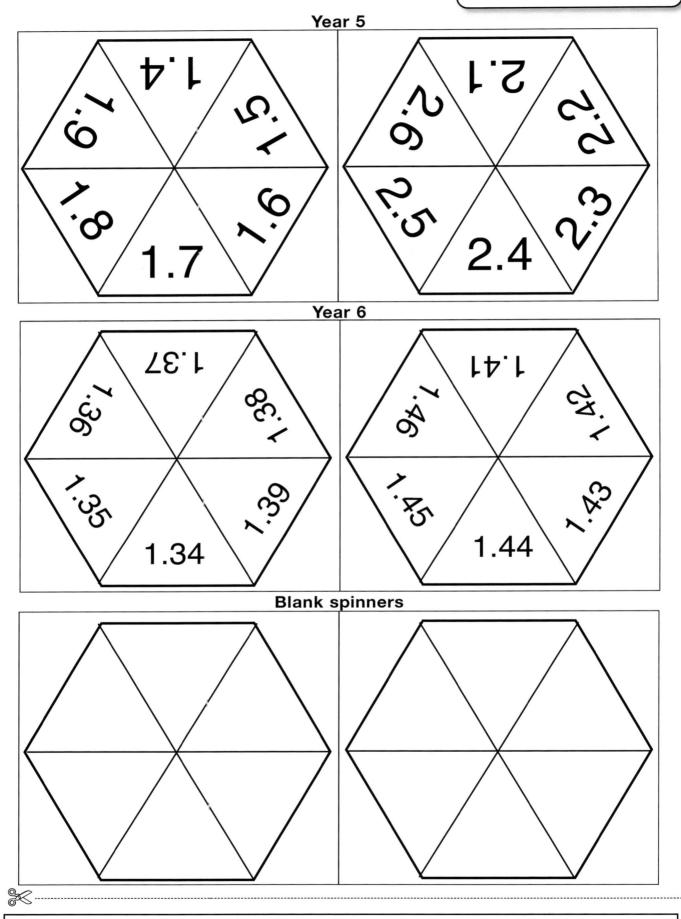

Year 6

Blank spinners

Notes for teachers: These spinners with numbers are for use with the objectives for Year 5 and 6 as outlined on pages 30 and 31. The blank spinners are to be used as suggested in the variations and plenary session on page 31.

Ski race

Doubles and near doubles

This game helps children to identify doubles and near doubles.

A game for two to six players

Learning objectives

Year 2: Identify near doubles using doubles already known, for example 8 + 9 and 40 + 41.

Year 3: Identify near doubles using doubles already known, for example 80 + 81.

Year 4: Identify near doubles using doubles already known, for example 150 + 160.

Year 5: Identify near doubles using decimals, for example 1.5 + 1.6.

Year 6, 7 & 8: Identify near doubles; for example, 1.61 + 1.55.

What you need

- a game board (page 37)
- a recording sheet (page 38)
- a 1–6 dice
- counters
- pencil and paper for jottings
- children's rules (page 86)

How to play

Players take turns to throw a dice and move their counter along the ski slope by the number of spaces indicated. If they land on an odd number they must work out the two consecutive numbers that make up that odd number. They write the numbers they have chosen and the total on the record sheet. If they do this successfully, they can move on an extra space. However, if they can't work out the numbers, or if they land on an even number, they stay where they are until their next throw. Play continues until someone reaches the end of the ski slope. This player is the winner.

Introducing the game

Tell the children that they are going to play a game to help them learn to identify two consecutive numbers from an odd number (for example, the number 37 can be made up from the consecutive numbers 18 and 19). This, in turn, will help them to recognise near doubles. The aim is to be the first player to get their counter to the end of the ski slope.

Example for Year 3 objective

- ❏ Complete the game board with numbers as shown below.
- ❏ Player 1 throws a 2 and lands on 70. It is an even number, so they stay there.
- ❏ Player 2 throws 3, lands on 91 and is able to say that the near doubles totalling 91 are 45 and 46. Player 2 can therefore move on an extra space.
- ❏ Player 1 throws 6, lands on 31 and is able to say that the near doubles for this are 15 and 16. Player 1 moves on an extra space.

Game board

Example for Year 2 objective

❑ Complete the track with numbers as shown in Example 1.

Example 1 for Year 2

Game board

Example for Year 4 objective

❑ Complete the track with numbers as shown in Example 2.

Example 2 for Year 4

Game board

Example for Year 5 objective

❑ Complete the track with numbers as shown in Example 3.

Example for Year 6, 7 & 8 objective

❑ Give children a blank copy of the track and ask them to create a game where they have to find near doubles of numbers with tenths and hundredths. So if 2.63 is a number on the board, the two consecutive numbers are 1.31 and 1.32. Discuss what other meanings there might be for 'consecutive numbers' i.e. could 1.312 and 1.313 be consecutive and if so, which numbers would they need on their board?

Example 3 for Year 5

Game board

Plenary session

❑ Write on the board a selection of odd numbers. Ask the children to work out as quickly as possible the two consecutive numbers that total them. This is self-differentiating if you write about eight numbers, beginning with some single- and two-digit numbers below 20 and progressing to other numbers up to 20 or 100. Ask the children to explain how they came up with the two numbers. Did they halve the nearest even number to give a starting point, for example? *What did you mean by 'consecutive number' in your game? What if you had a different meaning?*
(See Year 6, 7 & 8 example.)

Game board

Start

Recording Sheet

Name_____	
Number landed on	**2 consecutive numbers**

Name_____	
Number landed on	**2 consecutive numbers**

Name_____	
Number landed on	**2 consecutive numbers**

Join the numbers

Addition and subtraction by adjusting

This game helps children to add or subtract using a multiple of 10 and adjusting.

A game for two to four players

Learning objectives

Year 2: Add/subtract 9 or 11 by adding/subtracting 10 and adjusting by 1.

Year 3: Add/subtract mentally a near multiple of 10 to a two-digit number.

Year 4: Add or subtract the nearest multiple of 10, then adjust.

Year 5: Add or subtract the nearest multiple of 10 or 100, then adjust.

Years 6, 7 & 8: Add or subtract the nearest multiple of 10, 100 or 1000, then adjust.

What you need

- a 100 grid (Generic sheet 2) or decimal number grid (Generic sheet 3)
- felt-tipped pens
- 20 number cards (Generic sheets 4 to 14 to suit the children)
- spinners (page 41)
- children's rules (page 86)

How to play

Players use number cards to suit their achievement, such as two-digit numbers for Year 3, 4 and 5 and decimal cards for Year 6, 7 and 8. From a face-down pile of number cards, they take turns to pick a card, spin the spinner and perform the appropriate calculation. So, if they pick 34 and spin +9, they need to add 9 to 34 by adding 10 and adjusting. Encourage jottings, for example on number lines. They then have to draw in their own coloured felt-tipped pen the moves on their 100 squares, in this case joining the numbers 34, 44 and 43, to form an L-shape. After each turn, the card is put at the bottom of the pile. At the end of an agreed time, the winner is the player with the most numbers joined together with their colour.

Introducing the game

Tell the children that they are going to play a game that will help them to learn to add and subtract mentally by adding or subtracting 10 and then adjusting by 1. The aim is to join together as many numbers as possible on a number square.

Example for Year 3 objective

- ❑ These children should use the relevant spinner from page 41 and random two-digit cards. This is more challenging than the game for Year 2 as it includes +19, −19, +21 and −21.
- ❑ Player 1 picks 75 and spins −11, so draws the move 75, 65, 64.
- ❑ Player 2 picks 60, spins +19. He mentally adds 20, subtracts 1 and draws the move 60, 80, 79 on his 100 grid.
- ❑ Player 1 picks 9 and spins +21, so draws the move 9, 29, 30.
- ❑ Player 2 picks 98 and spins + 9, but can't draw the move because the numbers on the grid only go up to 100.
- ❑ Player 1 picks 42, spins −9, and draws the move 42, 32, 33.

And so on.

Player 1's 100 square would look like the one shown at the top of the facing page.

Player 1's completed grid in the game for Year 3 (see previous page).

1	2	3	4	5	6	7	8	9	10
11	12	13	14	15	16	17	18	19	20
21	22	23	24	25	26	27	28	29	30
31	32	33	34	35	36	37	38	39	40
41	42	43	44	45	46	47	48	49	50
51	52	53	54	55	56	57	58	59	60
61	62	63	64	65	66	67	68	69	70
71	72	73	74	75	76	77	78	79	80
81	82	83	84	85	86	87	88	89	90
91	92	93	94	95	96	97	98	99	100

Example for Year 2 objective

❏ These children should use the relevant spinner on page 41. This only uses the numbers 9 and 11 for addition/subtraction.

Example for Year 4 objective

❏ Let these children use either the Year 3 spinner or the Year 4 spinner on page 41. So, these children will be using the numbers 9, 11, 19, 21, 8 and 12 for addition/subtraction.

Example for Year 5 objective

❏ These children can use the Year 5 spinner which includes numbers from the Years 3 and 4 spinners. Alternatively they can use the decimal spinner and Generic sheet 3 as the game board. In this case they need the decimal cards on Generic sheet 12 or 13.

Example for Year 6, 7 & 8 objective

❏ These children can use the Year 6 spinner and the decimal game board on Generic sheet 3 for addition/subtraction of decimal numbers. The cards need to be decimals; for example, a selection from 1.1 to 8.9 and use either spinner on page 41.

Plenary session

❏ Ask the children to explain and demonstrate the calculation strategies they have been using. Progress to thinking about what would happen if you wanted to add or subtract 12 or 22 to a number. Demonstrate this by drawing the moves on a 100 grid.

❏ Explain why this method of adding and subtracting is important. Ask *Do you like this method for mental calculation?*

Year 2

Year 3

Year 4

Year 5

Year 5

Year 6, 7 & 8

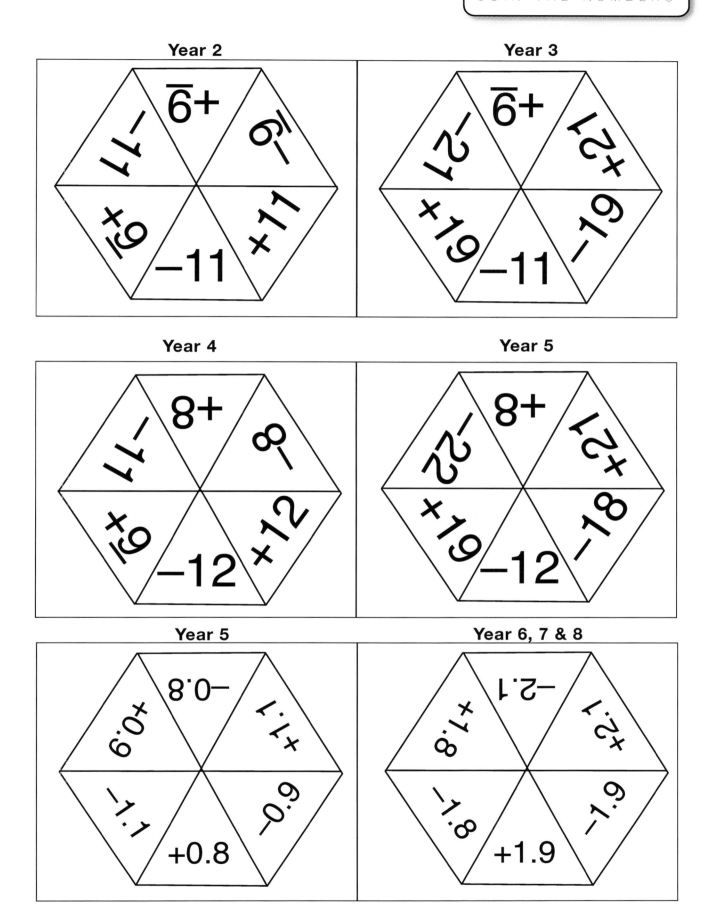

Hungry penguins

Addition and subtraction – inversions

A game for two to six players

Learning objectives

Year 2: Extend understanding that subtraction is the inverse of addition.
Year 3: Extend understanding that subtraction is the inverse of addition.
Year 4: Consolidate understanding of relationship between + and −.
Years 5, 6 & 7: Consolidate understanding and extend to decimals.

What you need

- a game board for each player (page 44)
- number cards (Generic sheets 4–13)
- fish counters (Generic sheet 18)
- paper and pencils
- timer or stopwatch
- children's rules (page 87)

This game helps children to understand that subtraction is the inverse of addition.

How to play

The aim of the game is for the children to win the most 'fish' for their penguin. Using the relevant numbers cards for the children's attainment (see Generic sheets 4 to 13), the cards are placed face down on the table. Player 1 turns over the top two cards. All the players find and write down as many addition and subtraction calculations as possible using the two numbers. Allow them one/two minutes for this, then ask them to count up and check each other's answers. The player with the most correct calculations scores that number of counters (fish) to put in their penguin's bucket. If there is a draw, the players with the same number of calculations both win fish. The cards are replaced at the bottom of the pack, Player 2 picks two more cards and the game continues. The winner is the player with the most fish in their penguin's bucket at the end of the session.

Introducing the game

Tell the children that this game will help them to learn about the relationship between addition and subtraction. The aim is to make up as many addition and subtraction calculations as possible to win fish counters to place in the penguins' buckets. Demonstrate the game with two numbers to suit your group.

Example for Year 3 objective

❑ Using the cards from Generic sheet 6 with numbers from 5 to 95 that are multiples of 5, place the cards face down on the table.
❑ Player 1 turns over the top two cards which are 15 and 60. These two numbers **must** be in every calculation.
❑ Within a time limit of one minute, all the players find and write down as many addition and subtraction calculations as possible using the two numbers.
❑ Once the allocated time is up, one child has the most calculation as follows:

$$15 + 60 = 75 \qquad 60 + 15 = 75 \qquad 60 - 15 = 45$$
$$60 - 45 = 15 \qquad 45 + 15 = 60 \qquad 15 + 45 = 60$$
$$75 - 60 = 15$$

❑ This player therefore wins seven fish for the penguins and puts the fish in her bucket.

Example for Year 2 objective

❏ These children should use the cards 0–20 on Generic sheets 4 and 5. So, if 9 and 3 are picked, number sentences could be:

$9 + 3 = 12$
$3 + 9 = 12$
$12 - 3 = 9$
$12 - 9 = 3$
$12 = 9 + 3$
$12 = 3 + 9$

Example for Year 4 objective

❏ Let these children use the cards 5–95 in multiples of 5 (Generic sheet 6) as well as random one- and two-digit numbers (Generic sheets 4, 5 and 7–9).

Example for Years 5, 6 and 7 objective

❏ Use random decimal numbers 0.1 to 9.9 (Generic sheets 12 and 13).

Variations

❏ Play without the game board and score 1 for every calculation and 10 for any correct calculation that no-one else has.

Plenary session

❏ Discuss the game with the children. Select two cards and ask them to give you as many calculations as possible using the two numbers. You will need to decide if you allow $9 + 3 = 12$ to be counted as different from $12 = 9 + 3$. It can be helpful to allow both versions to be counted because it alerts children to the real meaning of $=$ and helps them to think more creatively about number sentences. Discuss the inversion aspect of the session, relating the addition and subtraction relationship. Put some calculations such as $13 + \boxed{} = 24$ and $\boxed{} - 6 = 15$ on the board and ask the children how they can use their knowledge of inversions to work out the answer quickly.

❏ An alternative plenary activity could be to discuss how this relates to x and ÷. For example, say *If 6 x 7 = 42 what else can you tell me?*

❏ Ask *What was "new knowledge" for you today?*

Game boards

Notes for teachers: This page contains four game boards. Each player only needs one of them.

Game 12

Fishy matching

Addition and subtraction – Inversions

A game for groups of two to four players

Learning objectives

Year 2: Extend understanding that subtraction is the inverse of addition.
Year 3: Extend understanding that subtraction is the inverse of addition.
Year 4: Consolidate understanding of relationship between + and −.

What you need

- a game board (pages 47–49)
- two copies of the fish calculation cards (pages 50–52)
- Generic sheet 18
- counters
- children's rules (page 87)

> This game helps children to understand that subtraction is the inverse of addition.

How to play

Using the relevant cards for the year group objectives, place the cards face down in a pile. Let the children take it in turns to pick a card from the pile and see if they can find a calculation on the game board that is equivalent, but is not identical. (The calculation should contain the same three numbers but not in the same calculation.) If the calculation on the card is the equivalent of one on the game board, the child can cover it with a counter. If not, play passes to the next child. After each turn the cards should be put to the bottom of the pile. The game ends when all the calculations are covered and the winner is the player with the most counters on the game board.

Introducing the game

Tell the children that this game will help them to learn about the relationship between addition and subtraction. Explain that the aim is to cover – with counters – as many of the sums (or equations) on the game board as possible.

Example for Year 3 objective

❏ Players use Game board 2 on page 48 and the Calculation cards on page 51.
❏ Player 1 picks a card that reads $134 + 125 = 259$. There are three matches to this: $259 − 134 = 125$; $125 + 134 = 259$ and $259 − 125 = 134$. Player 1 decides to cover $125 + 134 = 259$ with a counter.
❏ Player 2 picks a card that reads $344 + 312 = 656$. There are three matches to this: $312 + 344 = 656$; $656 − 344 = 312$ and $656 − 312 = 344$. She decides to cover $656 − 344 = 312$ with her counter.
❏ During the game the same calculation will appear again. The number of match options will decrease as they are covered.

Example for Year 2 objective

❑ These children should use Game board 1 on page 47 and the Calculation cards 1 on page 50.

Example for Year 4 objective

❑ These children should use Game board 3 on page 49 and the Calculation cards 1 and 2 on pages 50 and 51.

Variations

❑ Using the blank fish cards on Generic sheet 18 and the blank game board on page 52, challenge the children to make their own game with different numbers.

Plenary session

❑ Ask the children how they worked out the matches. Write sets of three numbers on the board (such as 24, 32 and 56). Ask them to think of as many calculations as they can using all three. (The possible calculations are $24 + 32 = 56$, $32 + 24 = 56$, $56 - 24 = 32$ and $56 - 32 = 24$.)

❑ After doing this, write up another set of three numbers, such as 9, 4 and 36. Ask the children what calculations they can make up out of these. Making the link between inversion in + and – and x and ÷ is important and helps the children's understanding.

Game board – 1

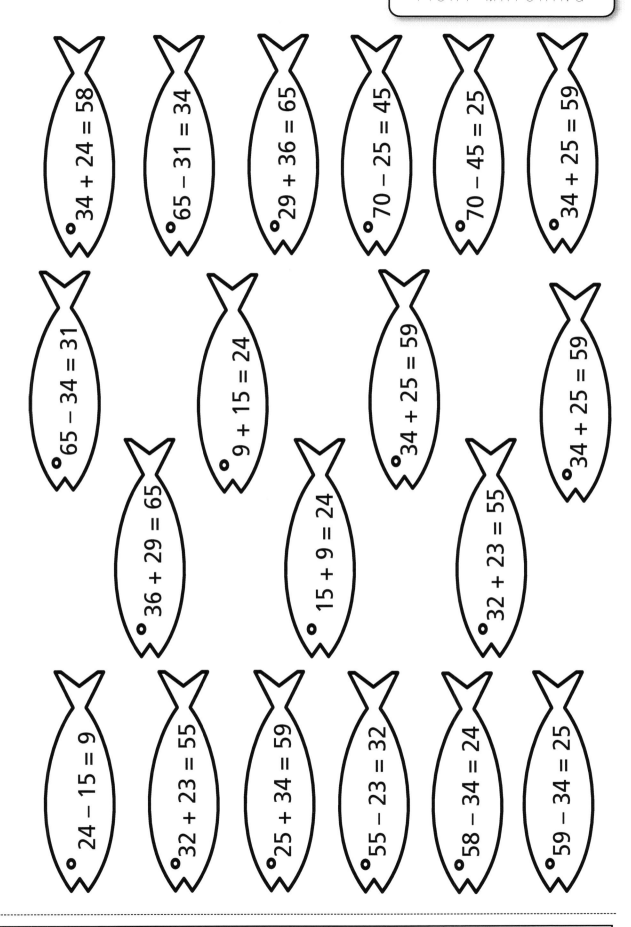

$34 + 24 = 58$

$65 - 31 = 34$

$29 + 36 = 65$

$70 - 25 = 45$

$70 - 45 = 25$

$34 + 25 = 59$

$65 - 34 = 31$

$9 + 15 = 24$

$34 + 25 = 59$

$34 + 25 = 59$

$36 + 29 = 65$

$15 + 9 = 24$

$32 + 23 = 55$

$24 - 15 = 9$

$32 + 23 = 55$

$25 + 34 = 59$

$55 - 23 = 32$

$58 - 34 = 24$

$59 - 34 = 25$

Notes for teachers: This game board is for use together with the cards on page 50 for the objective for Year 2.

Game board – 2

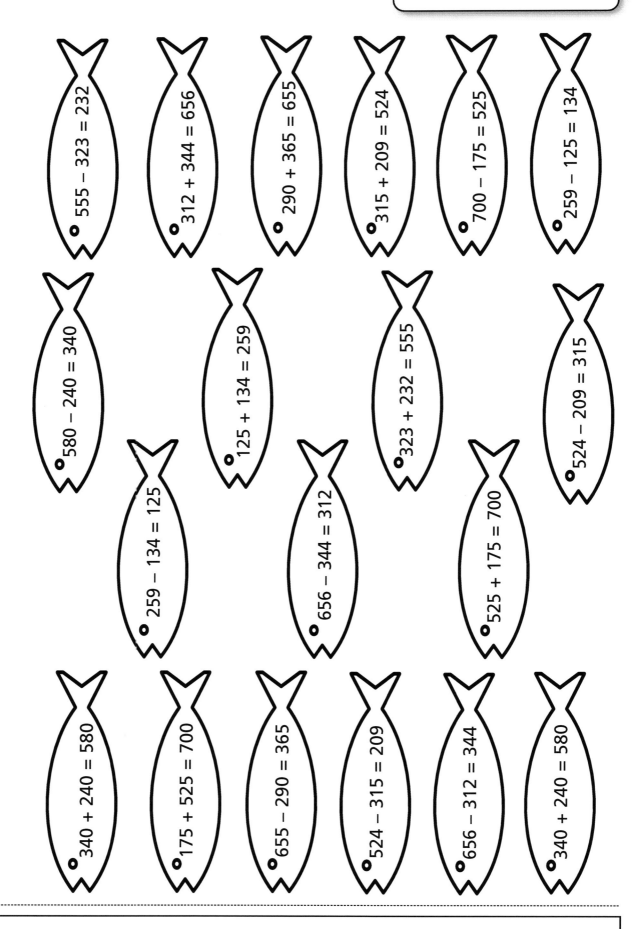

555 – 323 = 232

312 + 344 = 656

290 + 365 = 655

315 + 209 = 524

700 – 175 = 525

259 – 125 = 134

580 – 240 = 340

125 + 134 = 259

323 + 232 = 555

524 – 209 = 315

259 – 134 = 125

656 – 344 = 312

525 + 175 = 700

340 + 240 = 580

175 + 525 = 700

655 – 290 = 365

524 – 315 = 209

656 – 312 = 344

340 + 240 = 580

Notes for teachers: This game board is for use together with the cards on page 51 for the objective for Year 3.

Game board – 3

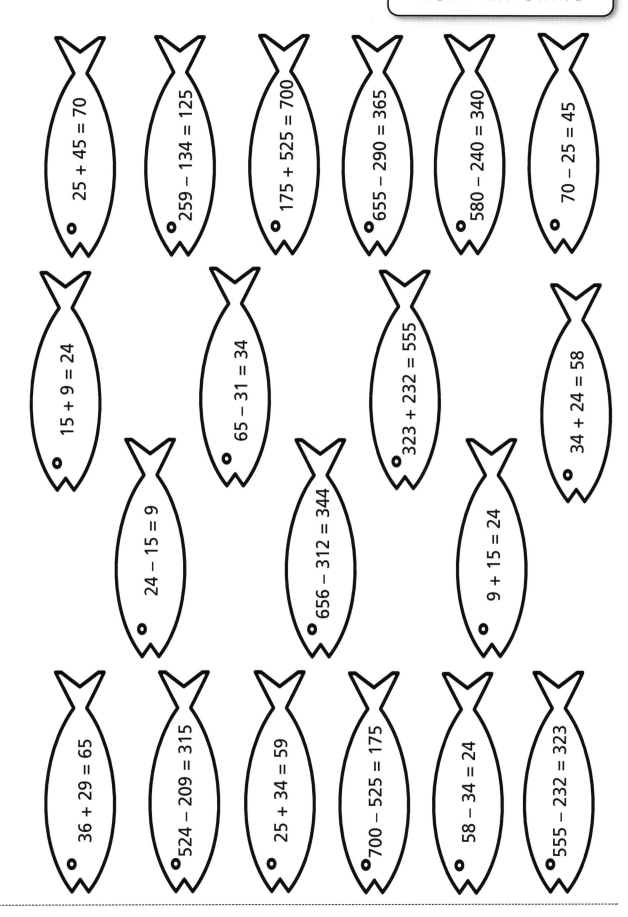

25 + 45 = 70

259 – 134 = 125

175 + 525 = 700

655 – 290 = 365

580 – 240 = 340

70 – 25 = 45

15 + 9 = 24

65 – 31 = 34

323 + 232 = 555

34 + 24 = 58

24 – 15 = 9

656 – 312 = 344

9 + 15 = 24

36 + 29 = 65

524 – 209 = 315

25 + 34 = 59

700 – 525 = 175

58 – 34 = 24

555 – 232 = 323

Notes for teachers: This game board is for use together with the cards on pages 50 and 51 for the objective for Year 4.

Calculation cards – 1

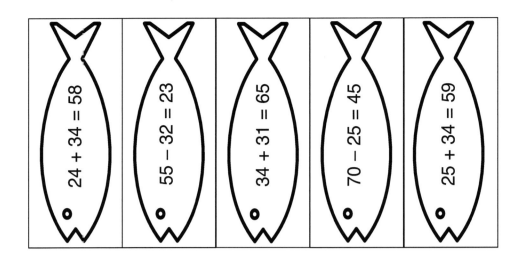

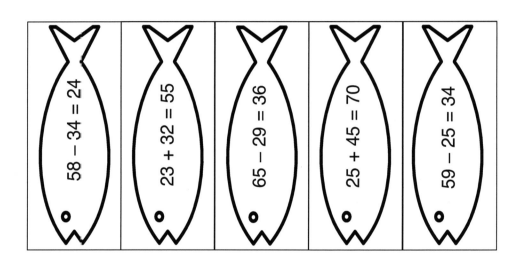

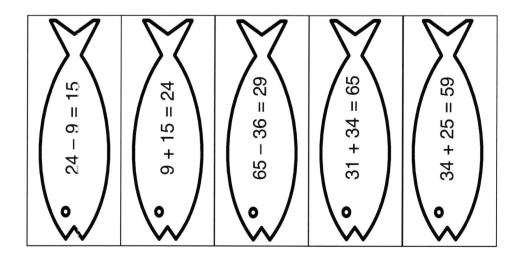

Notes for teachers: These cards are for use with the game board on page 47 for the objectives for Year 2 and with the cards on page 51 and the game board on page 49 for Year 4.

Calculation cards – 2

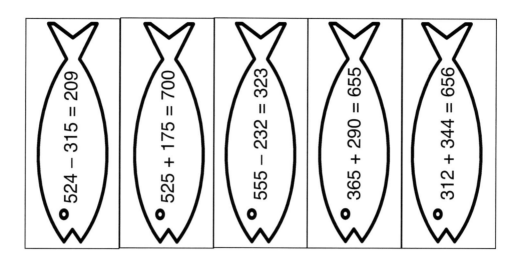

524 − 315 = 209   525 + 175 = 700   555 − 232 = 323   365 + 290 = 655   312 + 344 = 656

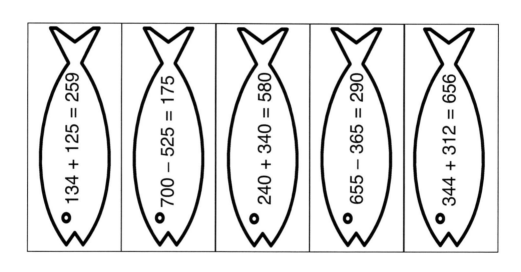

134 + 125 = 259   700 − 525 = 175   240 + 340 = 580   655 − 365 = 290   344 + 312 = 656

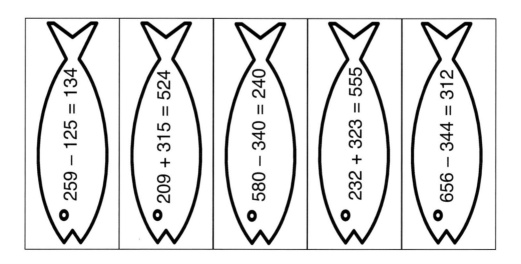

259 − 125 = 134   209 + 315 = 524   580 − 340 = 240   232 + 323 = 555   656 − 344 = 312

Notes for teachers: These cards are for use with the game boards on pages 48 and 49 for the objectives for Years 3 and 4. For Year 4 use the cards on this page and page 50.

Blank game board

MATHS GAMES **ADDITION AND SUBTRACTION – Book 2**

Game 13

Post it!

Which strategy?

> This game helps children to understand that subtraction is the inverse of addition.

A game for two players

Learning objectives

Year 3: Choose and use appropriate ways of calculating.
Year 4: Choose and use efficient calculation strategies.
Year 5, 6, 7, & 8: Choose and use appropriate ways of calculating.

What you need

- a game board (page 55)
- calculation cards (pages 56 to 61)
- recording sheet (page 62)
- pencils
- number lines
- blank calculation cards (page 63)
- children's rules (page 88)

How to play

Using the relevant calculation cards, players place the pile of cards face down beside the game board. They take turns to pick a 'letter' (calculation card), read it out to their partner and discuss the best method of solving the calculation. They then need to note the calculation on their recording sheet, and place the calculation card on the board by the dwelling that has that particular strategy. The game continues until all the mail has been delivered.

Introducing the game

This is a collaborative game rather than a competitive one. Explain to the children that they will be working in pairs pretending that they are postmen or women delivering letters to different homes. While playing the game, they will need to think about all the strategies for addition and subtraction that they have been working on and decide which one is the most efficient for a particular calculation. Emphasise specific ways of recording. For example, in one session you could ask for recording to be done on an empty number line while another time you might ask for all recording to be horizontal, or a mixture of horizontal and vertical.

Example for Year 3 objective

- ❑ Use the game board and the calculation cards on pages 56 and 57.
- ❑ The players take 203 − 196.
- ❑ They decide the best strategy is to count on from 196 to 203.
- ❑ They record their work as: 196 + 4 + 3 = 203, so the answer is 7.
- ❑ They then deliver the letter to dwelling number 3 because they have been finding a small difference by counting on.
- ❑ Then they pick another letter (card) which is 43 + 40 + 12.
- ❑ This time they decide the best strategy is to find pairs totalling multiples of 10.
- ❑ They record their work:
    40 + 40 + 10 = 50.   3 + 2 = 5.   50 + 5 = 55.
- ❑ They deliver the letter to dwelling number 5.

And so on.

Example for Year 4 objective

❏ These children should use the Calculation cards 3 and 4 on pages 58 and 59.

Example for Years 5, 6, 7 and 8 objective

❏ These children should use all the Calculation cards on pages 60 and 61.

Variations

❏ You can make a much easier game choosing just two homes and focus on two different strategies, using relevant calculations you have made using the blank letters (cards) on page 63.

❏ Play the game the other way round by giving the children the blank calculation cards and asking them to write a letter for each type of dwelling.

Plenary session

❏ Discuss the children's strategies for answering the calculations. Ask the rest of the class if they agree or if they would have chosen another strategy. Enlarge a game board and cut out the houses. Stick them on the board with sticky-tack. Have some letters prepared in advance. Invite the children to come out to the front and 'post a letter', justifying their decision each time.

❏ Alternatively, after sticking the houses on the board ask the children to make their own 'letters' for a house. Invite some of them to come out to the front of the class and show their letters, justifying why they belong to the particular houses chosen.

❏ Say, *Write a letter to go to this house. Why do you think that calculation belongs in that house? Who would do that a different way?*

❏ Ask *'Are some calculation strategies easier for you? Which strategies did you find the most difficult?'*

Game board

1

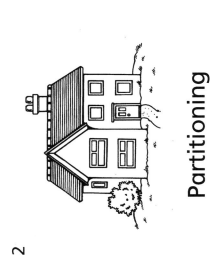

Near doubles

2

Partitioning

3

Find a small difference by counting on

4

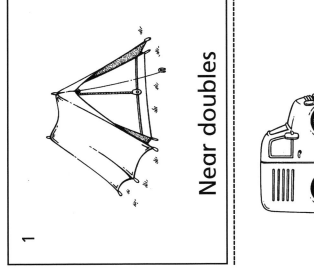

Rounding to the nearest 10 and adjusting

5

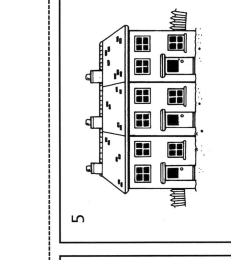

Finding pairs totalling 10, 20, 100 or a whole number.

6

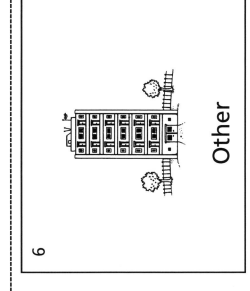

Other

Calculation cards – 1

80 + 81	60 + 61
50 + 51	30 + 31
90 + 91	40 + 41
34 + 54	27 + 42
33 + 65	46 + 52
63 + 42	72 + 34
102 – 97	106 – 95
203 – 196	92 – 85
205 – 199	89 – 78

Notes for teachers: These cards are for use with the Year 3 objectives.

Calculation cards – 2

36 + 19	87 + 19
64 + 19	52 – 19
72 – 19	65 – 19
9 + 6 + 4 + 3	8 + 4 + 5 + 2
12 + 7 + 8 + 3	5 + 4 + 15 + 6
9 + 7 + 11 + 13	18 + 8 + 2 + 2
17 + 17 + 10	100 – 36
43 + 40 + 12	67 – 13
96 + 103	237 + 165

Notes for teachers: These cards are for use with the Year 3 objectives.

POST IT!

Calculation cards – 3

150 + 160	120 + 130
170 + 160	110 + 120
140 + 150	100 + 110
134 + 154	117 + 141
143 + 155	126 + 153
263 + 142	272 + 234
1002 – 197	1006 – 198
2003 – 1996	2012 – 1999
2005 – 1991	4009 – 3998

Notes for teachers: These cards are for use with the Year 4 objectives.

Calculation cards – 4

96 + 39	187 + 99
164 + 28	252 – 49
352 – 38	265 – 88
19 + 60 + 40 + 3	80 + 14 + 25 + 20
12 + 70 + 28 + 30	50 + 40 + 50 + 60
90 + 70 + 11 + 30	180 + 80 + 20
145 + 187	267 – 187
289 + 178	208 – 125
387 + 289	247 – 82

Notes for teachers: These cards are for use with the Year 4 objectives.

Calculation cards – 5

1.5 + 1.6	2.3 + 2.4
3.4 + 3.5	4.2 + 4.3
4.3 + 4.4	5.1 + 5.2
1234 + ☐ = 2000	1142 + ☐ = 2222
1542 + ☐ = 999	2111 + ☐ = 3000
4324 + ☐ = 3999	3478 + ☐ = 5000
8006 – 2993	5006 – 195
6003 – 1996	9002 – 3995
2005 – 1996	7009 – 6994

Notes for teachers: These cards are for use with the Years 5, 6, 7 and 8 objectives.

Calculation cards – 6

3.6 + 1.9	8.7 + 1.9
6.4 + 2.1	5.2 – 2.8
7.2 – 3.1	6.5 – 4.9
1.7 + 1.3 + 2.9	1.8 + 2.4 + 3.2
6.4 + 3.2 + 1.8	7.5 + 2.1 + 4.5
4.9 + 3.1 + 6.3	1.8 + 4.8 + 1.2
4567 – 1254	4578 + 342
3678 – 1987	5987 + 1982
1987 – 287	4009 + 2765

Notes for teachers: These cards are for use with the Years 5, 6, 7 and 8 objectives.

Recording sheet

My letter	The strategy I chose	The calculation
Example: 203 – 196	Counting on	196 + 4 + 3 = 203

Blank calculation cards

Spinner 1

Spinner 2

Spinner 3

Spinner 4

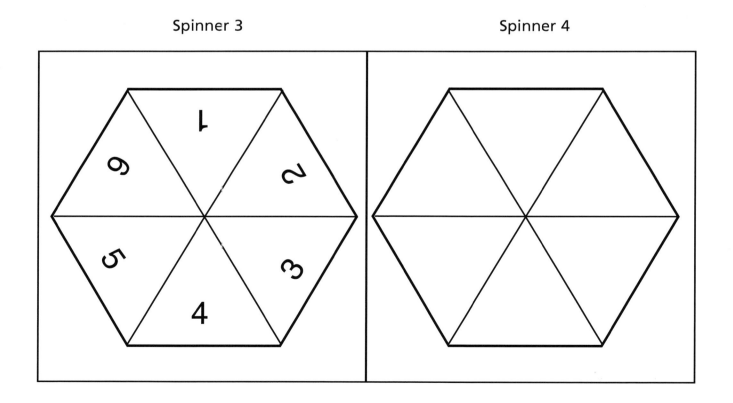

1	2	3	4	5	6	7	8	9	10
11	12	13	14	15	16	17	18	19	20
21	22	23	24	25	26	27	28	29	20
31	32	33	34	35	36	37	38	39	30
41	42	43	44	45	46	47	48	49	40
51	52	53	54	55	56	57	58	59	50
61	62	63	64	65	66	67	68	69	60
71	72	73	74	75	76	77	78	79	70
81	82	83	84	85	86	87	88	89	80
91	92	93	94	95	96	97	98	99	100

1	0.9	0.8	0.7	0.6	0.5	0.4	0.3	0.2	0.1
2	1.9	1.8	1.7	1.6	1.5	1.4	1.3	1.2	1.1
3	2.9	2.8	2.7	2.6	2.5	2.4	2.3	2.2	2.1
4	3.9	3.8	3.7	3.6	3.5	3.4	3.3	3.2	3.1
5	4.9	4.8	4.7	4.6	4.5	4.4	4.3	4.2	4.1
6	5.9	5.8	5.7	5.6	5.5	5.4	5.3	5.2	5.1
7	6.9	6.8	6.7	6.6	6.5	6.4	6.3	6.2	6.1
8	7.9	7.8	7.7	7.6	7.5	7.4	7.3	7.2	7.1
9	8.9	8.8	8.7	8.6	8.5	8.4	8.3	8.2	8.1
10	9.9	9.8	9.7	9.6	9.5	9.4	9.3	9.2	9.1

0	1	2	3
4	5	<u>6</u>	7
8	<u>9</u>	0	1
2	3	4	5
<u>6</u>	7	8	<u>9</u>

10	11	12	13
14	15	16	17
18	19	20	

5 - 95 in multiples of 5

5	10	15	20
25	30	35	40
45	50	55	60
65	70	75	80
85	90	95	

Random two-digit numbers

36	43	39	22
23	35	28	33
56	49	48	61
47	62	59	52
54	37	45	60

Random two-digit numbers

97	23	91	79
89	61	84	46
78	22	72	28
67	33	66	34
52	48	57	43

Random two-digit numbers

16	78	22	72
28	67	33	97
91	89	11	84
66	34	52	48
57	43	13	59

Random three-digit numbers

159	201	184	206
187	204	215	202
199	196	208	205
203	194	211	190
213	169	174	189

Random four-digit numbers

1998	2011	4997	5010
2996	3010	1987	2001
2989	3007	3995	4010
3990	4005	1996	2012
1989	1994	2997	4008

Random decimals

3.6	3.4	7.1	2.7	4.6
6.4	6.6	2.9	7.3	5.4
3.8	3.4	2.1	2.7	1.8
1.2	1.6	2.9	2.3	3.2
0.9	0.8	0.7	0.6	0.5
0.1	0.2	0.3	0.4	0.5

Random decimals

3.6	4.3	3.9	2.2	2.3
3.5	2.8	3.3	5.6	4.9
4.8	6.1	4.7	6.2	5.7
5.2	1.7	1.8	3.7	4.2
5.5	6.9	2.9	3.1	5.8
6.4	2.7	3.2	4.1	5.1

Two places of decimals

0.14	0.95	0.28	0.82	0.37
0.16	0.91	0.25	0.83	0.36
1.27	3.82	1.66	3.41	2.97
1.23	3.89	1.62	3.44	2.95
6.42	3.64	6.68	3.41	2.91
7.12	7.32	2.78	5.38	4.69

Blanks for decimals

Place value cards

Place value cards

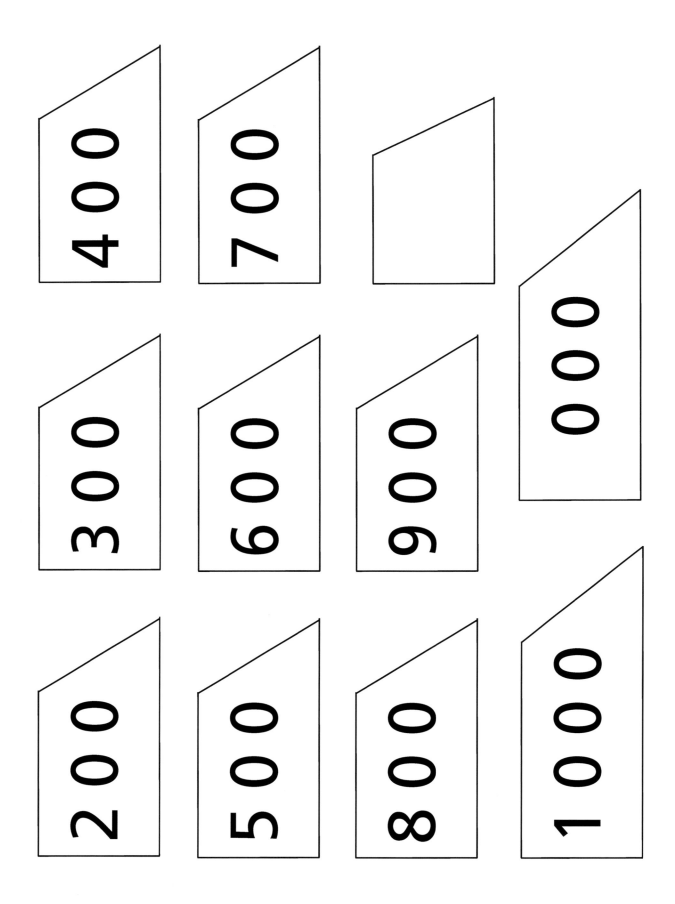

Blank number cards

Shape snakes

A game for two players. The aim is to do some additions to score the most points and make a picture of a snake.

You will need
- 10 shape cards each
- a recording sheet
- a pencil

How to play
- Take eight shape cards each. Don't look at the numbered side.
- Put the two remaining cards face up, side by side on the table.
- Player 1 puts a card beside them to start to form a snake shape and adds the three numbers together, putting the largest number first. If your total is ____, ____ or ____, score one point, and record it on the recording sheet.
- Player 2 puts a card beside the first player's and adds the total of that card and the previous two cards, gaining a point if the total is ____, ____ or ____ and recording the score.
- Player 1 repeats this, and play continues until all the cards have been used and you have made a snake shape.
- The winner is the player with the highest score.

Cover the numbers

A game for two to four players. The aim of this game is to perform additions and subtractions and cover as many squares as possible on your number square in the time you are given.

You will need
- a pile of counters, one colour for each player
- a game board
- + and – spinner
- number cards
- a timer

How to play
- Place the cards face down between you.
- Player 1 takes two cards, and performs an addition or subtraction with the cards, and looks for the answer on the game board. If the number is there it can be covered with a counter.
- The next player has a turn, but if the number has already been covered it cannot be used again. Also, if the number is not on the game board they cannot place a counter.
- Carry on in this way until your time is up.
- The winner is the player with the most counters on the game board at the end of the game.

Find the way

Rules

This is a game for two players. The aim of the game is to reach the finish, having scored the most points, by adding sets of _____ digit numbers together, two of which must total _____.

You will need

- counters
- a recording sheet
- pencils
- a game board
- a calculator

How to play

- Player 1 begins on the start square and, using that number, adds another _____ numbers onto it. Two of the numbers to be added must total _____ and all the numbers must be next to each other.
- Place your counters on the numbers, to help you remember which ones you chose.
- Write the numbers on your recording sheet beginning with the two that total _____. Your score is the total of your addition.
- Player 2 does the same thing but needs to take a different route.
- When one of you reaches the finish square, the game is over and you find your grand totals. You may use a calculator to do this. The winner is the player with the highest score.

Stars in your eyes

Rules

This is a game for two players or small groups. The aim is to cover all the numbers on your star with counters. The first player to do so is the winner.

You will need:

- a star game board
- game cards
- counters

How to play

- You will need a star game board each and the pack of number cards face down on the table.
- Fill each section of your star with numbers that your teacher tells you.
- Take it in turns to pick a card.
- Look at your card, and if it pairs up with one of your numbers to total _____, cover up that number with a counter.
- If you can't make a pair, the next player has their turn.
- After your go replace your card at the bottom of the pile.
- The winner is the first player to cover all their numbers on their star.

Rules

What's left?

This is a game for two to four players. The aim is to move around the course and get your counter home first.

You will need

- a game board
- counters
- game cards

How to play

- Place the game cards face down on the table in front of you, and put your counters on the 'start' square.
- Player 1 picks a card and then adds the single-digit number in the 'start' square to it by partitioning it into two numbers, to make the number on the card up to the next multiple of 10. For example, if you pick up a card with 47 on it, partition the 6 into 3 and 3, add the 3 to the 47 to make 50 and add the remaining 3 to make 53. The number that is the remaining number (in this case 3) is the number of moves you make around the board.
- Take it in turns to do this.
- If one of your additions does not leave a remaining number, you cannot move your counter.
- The winner is the first player home.

Rules

Hurdles

This is a game for two to six players. The aim is to jump the hurdles and win the race.

You will need

- place value cards
- addition/subtraction spinner
- a game board
- counters
- pencil and paper for jottings

How to play

- Put the sets of place value cards face down on the table in separate piles, ie the 10s in one pile. Put your counter on the start of your track.
- Each of you picks a place value card from each pile to make a number.
- Do this again to make a second number.
- Spin the + and − spinner. According to how it stops, you both add or subtract your two numbers.
- The player with the highest total or lowest difference jumps a hurdle on their race track by moving their counter along one space.
- When the cards have been used, shuffle them and play again.
- Carry on playing until someone wins the hurdle race.

Target numbers

Rules

This is a game for two to four players. The aim is to get your dart counter to the dartboard first.

You will need

- a game board
- target cards
- place value cards
- dart counters

How to play

- Place the pile of target cards face down on the table, and spread the place value cards out face down in front of you.
- Player 1 picks a target card, and everyone picks one of each place value card.
- Combine your cards to make a number.
- The player who has made the number closest to the target (either higher or lower) moves one space along the game board.
- If that player can tell everyone how close they are to the target number, they can move another space along the board.
- Put the cards back, mix them up and play again.
- The winner is the one whose dart counter reaches the target first.

Lost in space!

Rules

This is a game for two to six players. The aim of this game is to be the first player to get your spaceship back to Earth.

You will need

- a game board
- a number line
- two spinners
- spaceship counters

How to play

- Player 1 spins both spinners, then works out the difference between the two numbers by counting up from the lowest number, and moves their spaceship (counter) along the number of spaces that the difference came to.
- The next player then has a turn.
- Keep playing in this way. The first one to Earth is the winner.

Another option is to hit Earth exactly. So, if you have four spaces left between you and Earth and you spin a difference of 5, you can land on Earth and you have won. However, if you spin a difference of 8, you must move all eight spaces. So you move four forward, one space on to Earth and three spaces back along the track to make 8 moves. This means you now need to spin a difference of four to land on Earth.

Ski race

Rules

This is a game for two to six players. The aim is to be the first player to get their counter down the ski slope.

You will need

- a game board
- dice
- counters
- pencil and paper for jottings

How to play

- Take turns to throw the dice and move your counter the number of spaces indicated.
- If you land on an odd number, you must work out the two consecutive numbers that make up that odd number. If you can do so, write it on your recording sheet and then you can move on an extra space. If you can't do it because you land on an even number you stay where you are until your next throw.
- Carry on playing like this until one of you reaches the end of the ski slope. This player is the winner.

Join the numbers

Rules

This is a game for two to four players. The aim is to join together as many numbers as you can on your number grid.

You will need

- one 100 grid and one felt-tipped pen per player
- number cards
- + and – 9, 11, 19 and 21 spinners

How to play

- Place the pile of number cards face down in front of you.
- Take turns to pick a card from the pile, spin the spinner, and perform the calculation.
- Once you have performed the calculation, draw the moves on your 100 square by joining the numbers involved. So if you pick 34 and spin +19 you would join 34, 54 and 53.
- Replace your card at the bottom of the pile.
- Take it in turns to do this until your session is up.
- The winner is the player with the most numbers joined together.

Hungry penguins

Rules

This is a game for two to six players. The aim of this game is to make up as many addition and subtraction calculations as you can from just two numbers so that you can win fish to put in the penguin's bucket.

You will need

- one penguin per player
- number cards
- counters
- paper and pencils
- a timer or stopwatch

How to play

- Place the cards face down in a pile.
- Player 1 turns over the top two cards.
- Start the timer, and in the next two minutes everyone needs to make up as many addition and subtraction calculations as they can using the two numbers, and write them down on a piece of paper.
- At the end of your time, count up the answers and check each other's calculations.
- The player with the most correct calculations can put that number of 'fish' (counters) in their bucket.
- Put those cards at the bottom of the pack, and repeat the game again and again.
- The winner is the player with the most counters in their bucket at the end of the session.

Fishy matching

Rules

This is a game for groups of two to four players. The aim of this game is to cover as many 'sums' as you can with counters.

You will need

- a game board
- fish calculation cards
- counters

How to play

- Place the cards in a pile, face down on the table.
- Take it in turns to pick a card from the pile.
- Find a calculation that matches the card without being exactly the same, but telling the same number 'fact'.
- If you find one, cover it with a counter.
- The winner is the player with the most counters on the game board when it is filled.

Rules

Post it!

This is a game for two players. The aim is to find the best strategy for each calculation so that the 'letters' (calculation cards) can be delivered to the right houses on the game board.

You will need

- a game board
- letters (calculation cards)
- recording sheet
- pencil

How to play

- Place the game board in front of you and the letters in a pile face down beside it.
- Take turns to pick a letter and read out the calculation.
- Discuss which is the best strategy to solve the calculation.
- Use this strategy to work out the answer and record your working on the recording sheet.
- Deliver the letter to the right house on the game board.
- Keep playing until you have delivered all the letters.

Rules

The aim is to

You will need

-
-
-
-

How to play

-
-
-